Original title:

Waves of Trust

Author: Swan Charm

ISBN HARDBACK: 978-1-80560-285-9

ISBN PAPERBACK: 978-1-80560-750-2

Tranquil Depths of Reliability

In still waters, trust does flow,
Beneath the surface, soft and slow.
Waves of calm, a gentle sigh,
Anchored deep, where dreams rely.

The light above begins to dance,
As shadows weave a silent trance.
A promise held in every tide,
In tranquil depths, we confide.

Reflections in Solitude

In quiet corners, thoughts appear,
Echoes softly draw us near.
Mirrored moments, tender and shy,
In solitude, we learn to fly.

The gentle night wraps us in grace,
As we wander through this space.
Reflections deepen, shadows fall,
In solitude, we rise and call.

Shores of Sincerity

Where waves meet land, the truth does stand,
Gentle whispers in golden sand.
Hearts laid bare, with nothing to hide,
On shores of sincerity, we abide.

A tide of trust washes the shore,
Every heartbeat, we long for more.
In the light of day, our spirits soar,
On shores of sincerity, we explore.

Embracing the Current

With open arms, we greet the flow,
The river's song begins to grow.
In every bend, a tale untold,
Embracing the current, fierce and bold.

As waters surge and softly glide,
We find our peace in the wild ride.
No fear of where the waves may lead,
Embracing the current, we are freed.

The Compass of Shared Dreams

In twilight's glow, we find our way,
With whispers soft, our hearts convey.
Maps made of laughter, light as air,
Together we journey, a sacred pair.

Through uncharted lands, our spirits roam,
With hopes as anchors, we call it home.
Each shared dream a star, in night's embrace,
Guiding us onward, to destiny's place.

In storms, we stand, a steadfast crew,
With courage deep, and love so true.
Compasses forged from bonds we hold,
A voyage of stories, waiting to be told.

Every step echoes, our dreams aligned,
Paths interwoven, hearts intertwined.
In the silence, our souls ignite,
Illuminating paths, through darkest night.

A journey's treasure, not far or wide,
But in the moments where we confide.
With each sunrise, new dreams unfurl,
Together we dance, in this vast world.

Driftwood Dreams

Along the shore, where tides embrace,
Driftwood whispers, in nature's grace.
Each piece a tale, of journeys vast,
Hopes and memories, of love amassed.

Waves caress, with tender sighs,
Carrying secrets beneath soft skies.
In their rhythm, lost dreams reside,
Hiding within, the ocean's tide.

I gather fragments, stories untold,
In every curve, a promise bold.
The past may linger, like scent of pine,
But new horizons spark, yet to shine.

With every sunset, let go and feel,
Nature's canvas, becomes our reel.
Driftwood dreams, like us, will sway,
Chasing the dawn, through night to day.

In every grain, the world's embrace,
Life flows freely, in gentle grace.
Together we drift, on life's grand stream,
Finding our way, through driftwood dreams.

Paths Beyond the Waters

Beneath the sky, where rivers flow,
Lie hidden trails, we long to know.
With every ripple, stories rise,
Of journeys cherished, beneath the skies.

Casting reflections, the waters gleam,
Whispers of fate, weave through the dream.
In quiet moments, we will explore,
Paths beyond the waters, forevermore.

Footprints linger, on shores of yore,
In every wave, we hear the roar.
The call of adventure, our hearts' delight,
Guiding us onward, into the night.

With courage ignited, we dare to roam,
Through verdant meadows, we'll find our home.
Each step a testament, bonds that form,
Paths intertwining, in life's sweet norm.

Together we chase, the horizon's gleam,
Beyond each river, awaits a dream.
In unity found, our spirits soar,
Paths beyond the waters, forever more.

Calming the Waters Inside

In depths where silence dwells,
A gentle breeze begins to swell.
Ripples dance upon the skin,
Whispers guide the peace within.

Beneath the surface, shadows fade,
In tranquil pools, fears are laid.
The heart reflects the sky's embrace,
A soothing light, a warm trace.

Finding solace in the flow,
Each breath a wave, calm and slow.
The storms of thought no longer rage,
In stillness, I turn the page.

With every breath, the mind resets,
The inner chaos now forgets.
Embracing calm, I rest my soul,
In waters deep, I find my whole.

Serenity is mine to claim,
As ripples dance, I call my name.
In this cocoon, I am alive,
My spirit learns to gently thrive.

Trust Beyond the Shore

Waves crash lightly on the sand,
A promise waits, a guiding hand.
Beyond the edge where waters twine,
Trust beckons softly to be thine.

In every tide that ebbs and flows,
Is courage found that softly grows.
The horizon melts into the grey,
Yet faith remains, come what may.

With each swell that breaks anew,
I stand with heart, I stand with you.
Unseen depths hold tales untold,
In trust, our futures brightly unfold.

Adventure calls from distant lands,
Where dreams take flight and life expands.
Beyond the shore, we find our way,
In whispered hopes, we choose to stay.

Together we embrace the vast,
With every moment destined to last,
In waters deep, no fear to bore,
We sail as one, forevermore.

Echoing Through Time

In quiet glades of ancient trees,
Echoes linger on the breeze.
Whispers of the past entwined,
In every note, our souls aligned.

Memories dance like flickering light,
A symphony from day to night.
Time weaves tales, both strong and frail,
In every heartbeat, hear the trail.

Moments shared, a timeless song,
In echoes bright, we all belong.
The present holds the past's embrace,
In fleeting time, a lasting trace.

Each laughter shared, each tear we've cried,
A melody that won't subside.
Through the ages, we remain,
In harmony, we find our gain.

Together, we'll create the sound,
With every heartbeat, love profound.
As echoes fade, our spirits chime,
Connected deeply, through all time.

Harmonizing Hearts

In rhythm soft, our pulses meet,
A dance of souls, both light and sweet.
Melodies created, pure and bold,
In every note, our stories told.

With gentle hands, we weave a tune,
A symphony beneath the moon.
The world around us fades away,
In harmony, we choose to stay.

Voices rise like morning light,
Together, we ignite the night.
In every chord, a magic spark,
Our hearts aligned, igniting dark.

Through trials faced, our bond grows strong,
In every struggle, we belong.
Two hearts entwined, not torn apart,
In every beat, a brand-new start.

As laughter rings and joy takes flight,
We forge our path, our spirits bright.
In unison, we'll find our way,
In harmonies that love can play.

Gentle Currents of Faith

In the quiet flow of night,
Whispers of hope take their flight.
Stars above softly gleam,
Carrying dreams like a stream.

Through valleys deep and wide,
Faith serves as our gentle guide.
In shadows where fears reside,
We find strength at faith's side.

With each step upon the way,
Morning light brings a new day.
Clouds may gather, skies may grey,
Yet faith will never sway.

In the heart, a spark ignites,
Guiding us through darkest nights.
With courage, we face our plight,
Holding on with all our might.

Faith, a current ever near,
Cleansing doubt, replacing fear.
In its embrace, we persevere,
Finding peace, we stay sincere.

Tides of Assurance

Waves crash upon the shore,
Each one brings hope, evermore.
With the ebb and with the flow,
Certainty begins to grow.

The moon pulls the sea with grace,
In this dance, we find our place.
Anchored firm, we shall not drift,
In the tides, we find our gift.

Whispers rise from ocean deep,
Promises that gently keep.
Crashing tides do reassess,
Through each wave, we find success.

In the rhythm of the sea,
Assurance flows, setting us free.
Through storms that may trouble the heart,
We find strength in every part.

Safe we stand upon this ground,
In each wave, assurance found.
With each swell, we rise anew,
Tides of trust carry us through.

Echoes of Reliability

In the stillness of the morn,
Promises anew are born.
Echoes of a steadfast truth,
Guide us gently in our youth.

Through the fog and through the haze,
Reliability displays.
In the voices heard each day,
Words of trust lead the way.

With each heartbeat, steadfast sound,
In this rhythm, we are bound.
Walls may tremble, doubts may rise,
Yet reliability never lies.

In the moments when we falter,
Trusting hands can lift and alter.
Across the valleys deep and wide,
Reliability is our guide.

As we walk this path of life,
Through the joy and through the strife.
In our hearts, the echoes stay,
Reminding us, we're not astray.

Breezes of Confidence

Softly blow the morning air,
Whispers of confidence care.
Rising up, we feel the lift,
In the breeze, we find our gift.

With each gust that sweeps the ground,
Courage grows, we stand profound.
Breezes dance through fields of gold,
Telling tales of strength untold.

In sunlight, shadows are cast,
Confidence blooms, unsurpassed.
Through the trials, we shall soar,
With each breath, we seek for more.

Let the winds of change embrace,
Guiding us to our own place.
In each moment, we shall trust,
Confidence strong, like untrammeled gusts.

Hear the call of the wild air,
In its magic, we declare:
Through the breezes, dreams take flight,
Carried high on wings of light.

Flowing Streams of Integrity

In shadows deep where whispers lie,
The streams of truth flow gently by.
With every bend, they carve their fate,
A mirror clear, a soul's true state.

Through trials faced and paths uncharted,
The heart stands firm, steadfast, not parted.
In silent depths, a promise made,
To honor what cannot degrade.

The ripples dance on water's face,
Reflecting honor with serene grace.
Each drop a vow, each wave a song,
In flowing streams, the brave belong.

Roots entwine in soil so rich,
Anchoring faith in every pitch.
As seasons change, the waters gleam,
They guide us home, our steadfast dream.

So let us tread where honor calls,
In vale and hill, where justice falls.
A journey bold, forever true,
In flowing streams, we'll start anew.

The Dance of Conviction

Beneath the stars, a rhythm sways,
As courage leads, the heart obeys.
In every step, the spirit soars,
A dance of truth that ever roars.

With every leap, the doubt takes flight,
In shadows cast, we find our light.
Embracing challenges, we arise,
With fiery hope that never dies.

Together we whirl, a boundless dream,
In unity, we form the beam.
The floor of fate, our stage sublime,
With every heartbeat, we defy time.

Each twirl a pledge, each spin a prayer,
In the dance of life, we truly care.
With steadfast hearts and voices raised,
In conviction's arms, we're forever praised.

So let us sway to life's sweet song,
In every moment, know we belong.
The dance of conviction, fierce and free,
A joyful march to destiny.

Embracing the Unknown

In twilight's hush, the journey starts,
With open minds and tender hearts.
The path ahead, a mystery clear,
Where shadows whisper, love draws near.

We step with trust into the night,
Embracing fears, we seek the light.
Each twist and turn, a chance to grow,
In every step, the thrill unfolds.

The stars above, they guide our way,
With dreams like lanterns lit today.
In every heartbeat, courage found,
The unknown calls, a timeless sound.

As tides of time begin to sway,
We gather strength to brave the fray.
In certainties that fade away,
We bloom anew without delay.

So let us walk through life's great maze,
With faith as bold, we'll find our ways.
Embracing all that's yet to come,
In unknown arms, we are truly one.

Tidal Embrace

The ocean's breath, a soothing balm,
In waves that crash, we find a calm.
With every tide, a story told,
In salty air, our dreams unfold.

As currents pull with gentle might,
We seek the shore, a guiding light.
In every ebb, a lesson learned,
In tidal waves, our hearts have yearned.

The dance of water, soft and sweet,
In every splash, our lives compete.
Here we unite in nature's song,
With open arms, we all belong.

As seas expand, so do our souls,
With every surge, we become whole.
In tidal embrace, we face the storm,
Together weathered, forever warm.

So let us dive into the deep,
In ocean's arms, our promises keep.
Tidal embrace, our spirits soar,
A voyage vast, forevermore.

Resilience in Ripples

In the stillness, strength unfolds,
Small waves crash, stories told.
Fleeting moments, shadows cast,
Yet hope glimmers, steadfast vast.

Each drop echoes, a heart once torn,
From broken seeds, new dreams are born.
In every ripple, courage ignites,
Through storms and silence, inner lights.

Challenges loom, yet spirits soar,
Finding footing on life's shore.
With each crest, we maximize,
The beauty hidden in the rise.

Together we weather, the ebb and flow,
Healing waters, deep and slow.
What once was fear, now softly glows,
In resilience, our true strength shows.

Across the surface, calm and bright,
Emerging stronger, ready for flight.
For in the ripples, we arise,
Transforming trials into skies.

The Bridge of Unspoken Bonds

Between two hearts, a bridge is laid,
In silent whispers, truths conveyed.
No need for words, just knowing looks,
In timeless pages, we write our books.

Through trials faced, side by side,
A steady anchor, where love abides.
Moments shared, though words may flee,
In quiet gaps, we truly see.

Every glance, a silent song,
In every heartbeat, we belong.
Our spirits meld, like twinkling stars,
Obscured by distance, never far.

Through storms that try to pull apart,
Our bond endures, a work of art.
With faith like roots, we intertwine,
In unspoken love, our fates align.

Hand in hand, we walk the line,
In gentle strength, our hearts entwine.
For in the silence, loud and clear,
Our unyielding bond brings us near.

Safeguarded by Serenity

In the quiet, peace descends,
Softly wrapped in gentle bends.
A tranquil heart, a calming sigh,
Where burdens lift, and spirits fly.

Each moment cherished, each breath slow,
In stillness, the wild rivers flow.
Nestled deep in nature's arms,
We find refuge from worldly harms.

With every wave, a chance to heal,
A soothing presence, a quiet feel.
The world outside may rush and race,
But here, we carve our sacred space.

In whispered winds, wisdom flows,
A healing touch that softly glows.
Through storms that shake, we find our ground,
In serenity's arms, we are found.

Cocooned in stillness, we arise,
Beneath a canopy of skies.
With hearts aligned and spirits bright,
We walk in peace, embraced by light.

Shifting Tides of Confidence

The ocean's breath, a guiding force,
Beneath the waves, we chart our course.
With every shift, we learn to stand,
Embracing change, life's gentle hand.

In quiet depths, where shadows blend,
Confidence grows, fears begin to mend.
Each challenge faced, a lesson learned,
From flickering embers, our spirits burned.

With every tide, we learn to sway,
Finding strength in the dance of play.
Through rising waves, our spirits rise,
Understanding fear, yet claiming skies.

The currents shift, the patterns change,
In this flow, we foster range.
Trusting the rhythm, we find our way,
Guided by hope, come what may.

In shifting tides, we find our light,
With open hearts, we take to flight.
For every journey, a purpose clear,
In confidence, we shed the fear.

The Harmony of Hope

In the dawn's embrace, dreams ignite,
Soft whispers of light, banishing night.
A symphony blooms, in every heart,
Hope dances gently, a cherished art.

Through valleys of doubt, we rise anew,
Each step forward, a promise true.
Together we stand, hand in hand,
In the tapestry of life, beautifully planned.

Mountains may tower, storms may roar,
Yet hope is the beacon, forever more.
With every challenge, we find our way,
Guided by light, come what may.

The sky may darken, as shadows fall,
But hope is the echo, answering the call.
In the stillness, we forge our fate,
United in spirit, never too late.

So let the winds blow, let the rivers flow,
For in the heart's garden, hope will grow.
A melody sweet, through time it streams,
The harmony of hope, whispers our dreams.

Undercurrents of Dependability

In silent shadows, trust resides,
A constant anchor, where truth abides.
Roots intertwined, through earth so deep,
In the arms of time, promises keep.

Like a warm blanket, it wraps us tight,
Through darkest storms, it shines so bright.
A gentle whisper, a steadfast hand,
Dependability, our firm foundation stand.

With every falling star, our bonds grow strong,
In this symphony of life, we belong.
Through laughter and tears, we face the day,
In the dance of life, dependably, we sway.

Though tides may shift and tempests surge,
Our hearts united, a mighty merge.
In silent waters, we find our guide,
With undying faith, right by our side.

Together we weave, a tapestry grand,
In every heartbeat, we understand.
Dependability's grace will never tire,
An undercurrent of love, timeless fire.

Soothing Waters of Loyalty

In gentle streams, our promise flows,
With every ripple, our connection grows.
A sanctuary built on trust so pure,
In loyalty's embrace, we find our cure.

Through trials faced, we stand as one,
Beneath the moonlight, our journey begun.
Each whispered secret, a bond that ties,
In the soothing waters, true loyalty lies.

When shadows loom, and doubts arise,
The heart's true compass never lies.
In the depths of silence, we remain,
Soothing each other through joy and pain.

Like steadfast trees, we bend but don't break,
In the arms of loyalty, we find our stake.
Through storms we weather, together we stay,
In the soothing waters, we'll find our way.

With every heartbeat, loyalty sings,
A melody sweet, the comfort it brings.
In every moment, through thick and thin,
Soothing waters of loyalty, forever within.

Cascading Certainty

In the rhythm of time, certainty flows,
Like cascading waters, strong and slow.
A promise unspoken, steadfast and clear,
In the heart of chaos, it draws us near.

Mountains may crumble, and rivers may shift,
But certainty shines, a divine gift.
In the dance of life, we find our place,
With every heartbeat, we embrace grace.

Through shadows of doubt, it lights the way,
Guiding our steps, come what may.
A river of trust, in the depths profound,
In cascading certainty, we are found.

With every sunrise, we greet the day,
Grounded in truth, in every way.
Let waves crash loud, let the storms dare,
For in certainty's arms, we stand aware.

So let the waters flow, strong and free,
In cascading certainty, we're meant to be.
A tapestry woven, a bond so tight,
In the light of assurance, everything's right.

The Lighthouse of Faith

In storms it stands so tall and bright,
A guiding star in darkest night.
It whispers hope to weary hearts,
A flame that never, ever departs.

Through crashing waves and howling winds,
It keeps the loss from turning sins.
A beacon strong, through fear and doubt,
Its light will show what life's about.

With every prayer, its power grows,
A sanctuary where love flows.
Faith holds us through the strife and pain,
A promise made, it will remain.

In quiet moments, we find its grace,
A tender touch in a sacred space.
Through trials faced and burdens borne,
The lighthouse stands, our spirits worn.

When paths are dark, and hope seems lost,
It shines for all, regardless of cost.
A faithful guardian on the shore,
It calls us home to seek once more.

A Sea of Understanding

Beneath the waves, where secrets lie,
Compassion flows, like the open sky.
In every tide, a lesson learned,
In quiet depths, our hearts are turned.

With every swell, we come together,
A tapestry woven, light as feather.
Through storms we navigate, hand in hand,
Building bridges on this vast land.

In gentle waves, kindness reigns,
Through shared laughter, joy remains.
A deep embrace, where souls connect,
In this sea, we reflect and respect.

Like fish that swim in harmony,
We learn to thrive in community.
Each ripple holds a tale unique,
In this vast ocean, we all seek.

As the sun sets, colors blend,
In unity, we find our friends.
Together we float on currents strong,
In this sea of understanding, we belong.

Anchors of Belief

In life's tempestuous sea we stand,
With anchors firm, hand in hand.
They ground us when the waves arise,
A testament beneath the skies.

Each anchor holds a story dear,
Of moments shared, of laughter and cheer.
Through trials faced, they hold us tight,
In darkest days, they bring the light.

When storms assail and doubts collide,
These anchors serve as strength and guide.
They remind us of the love we share,
A promise made, a silent prayer.

With steadfast hearts, we rise and fall,
In unity, we answer the call.
For like the stars that light the night,
Our anchors shine and ward off fright.

So let us cherish through each plume,
The anchors deep that banish gloom.
In every storm, we find our peace,
Together bound, our joys increase.

The Architecture of Friendship

In bricks of trust, we build our space,
Each moment shared, a warm embrace.
With laughter as our sturdy beam,
We weave together every dream.

Like windows wide that let in light,
Our friendship's glow ignites the night.
Through trials faced, we do not wane,
In every storm, there's love to gain.

Each room a refuge, safe and sound,
Where secrets shared are always found.
In silence too, we find our peace,
In every heartbeat, bonds increase.

With open doors and hearts so true,
We cherish all that we pursue.
Architects of joy we'll always be,
In this grand structure, wild and free.

So let us paint with colors bright,
This masterpiece of shared delight.
Together always, through joy and strife,
The architecture of our life.

Harbor of Hope

In the distance, a beacon shines bright,
Guiding lost souls through the night.
Whispers of dreams on the breeze,
In this safe place, hearts find ease.

Waves lapping softly against the shore,
Promises linger, forevermore.
Anchored in faith, we stand tall,
In the harbor of hope, we won't fall.

Seagulls call with a knowing grace,
Reminding us of our own safe space.
With each tide, a new chance to start,
This sanctuary holds every heart.

The sun dips low, painting the sky,
A canvas of dreams, we reach for high.
Together we weather the fiercest storms,
Finding shelter in love, our hearts warm.

As the stars weave tales bright and clear,
The harbor of hope, forever near.
Through trials and tests, we remain strong,
In this haven, we all belong.

Echoes of Loyalty

In a world where whispers fade,
Loyal hearts never stray.
Through thick and thin, side by side,
In the warmth of trust, we abide.

Memories linger in the air,
Echoes of promises made with care.
Hand in hand, we brave the night,
Guided by stars, ever so bright.

Through valleys deep and mountains high,
Our bond remains, it will not die.
Like rivers flowing to the sea,
Loyalty anchors you and me.

In silence shared, words unspoken,
The ties of friendship are never broken.
With laughter ringing, hearts in tune,
Together we dance beneath the moon.

As seasons change and time rolls on,
The echoes of loyalty are never gone.
With every heartbeat, love's refrain,
In the depths of our souls, it will remain.

The Crest of Credence

On the summit where the eagles soar,
Lies the truth we all explore.
With courage as our guiding light,
We face our fears and take the flight.

Mountains rise and shadows cast,
But our dreams are built to last.
Together we climb, hand in hand,
Reaching heights, making our stand.

Through storms that rage and skies so gray,
Our faith will guide us along the way.
With every step, we gain our creed,
At the crest of credence, we plant our seed.

The winds may howl, but we are strong,
In the heart of unity, we belong.
With voices lifted in joyful song,
We find our place, we won't go wrong.

As the dawn breaks, anew we rise,
In this journey, we find our prize.
With every heartbeat, we take a chance,
At the crest of credence, the world's our dance.

Sheltering Shores

Where the ocean kisses the land,
Sheltering shores, so soft and grand.
In the embrace of the gentle tide,
We find a refuge, where dreams bide.

The whispers of waves bring tales untold,
Of love and courage, of hearts so bold.
Each grain of sand, a memory held,
In this sacred space, our spirits meld.

Sunrise paints the horizon wide,
In colors of hope, we take our stride.
Laughter dances on the breeze,
In the shelter of shores, we find our ease.

With each sunset, shadows blend,
In this haven, we transcend.
Together we weave our stories bright,
Under the canopy of stars at night.

As tides ebb and flow with grace,
This sanctuary is our sacred place.
On these shores, we stand so true,
In the shelter of love, I'm safe with you.

Navigating Truths

In shadows deep, we search for light,
Clasping hopes, our hearts take flight.
The map we seek is drawn within,
Guiding us through where doubts have been.

With every step, the path unfolds,
Stories told, and wisdom holds.
We wade through murky, uncertain streams,
Chasing whispers of distant dreams.

Each compass point leads us anew,
Trusting what feels honest and true.
A journey defined by twists and bends,
In unity, the soul transcends.

We gather fragments of our past,
In tides of time, they hold us fast.
Embracing change, we rise and dive,
Learning that in truth, we thrive.

So here we stand, hearts open wide,
Navigating with love as our guide.
In this vast sea, we find our worth,
Amidst the waves, we give birth.

Sailing into Certainty

With sails unfurled, we set our course,
Driven by a steadfast force.
Each wave that breaks, each swell we ride,
Brings us closer to what's inside.

The wind whispers secrets of the sea,
In every gust, a chance to be free.
Our compass points to the light ahead,
Guiding thoughts that once were shed.

The horizon calls, a beckoning song,
In these waters, we feel we belong.
We navigate through doubts and fears,
Charting paths with honest tears.

Every star above, a guiding light,
Illuminating the endless night.
As we sail, our spirits soar,
Firm in belief, we crave for more.

Together we rise, with hope in our sails,
Through storms we weather and curious gales.
Sailing into certainty, we find our way,
One heartbeat closer with each passing day.

The Estuary of Empathy

In gentle tides where rivers meet,
Understanding flows, so bittersweet.
Hearts entwined in the ebb and flow,
In silence, we learn what we don't know.

Each story whispered, a bridge we build,
With compassion deep, our spirits filled.
The currents tug at our very core,
Drawing us closer to the forgotten shore.

In reflections of sorrow and joy,
We embrace each other, the girl and boy.
In this estuary, we shed our pride,
Finding strength where love will abide.

Beneath the surface, life pulses bright,
In every choice, we claim our right.
To listen, to hold, and to understand,
In this sacred space, united we stand.

So let the waters wash over our souls,
Blurring the lines, making us whole.
In the estuary where feelings flow,
Empathy blooms, and together we grow.

Ripples of Belief

In tranquil pools, a stone is cast,
Ripples form, extending vast.
With every drop, a chain reaction,
Creating waves of profound attraction.

What we hold close, we share with care,
Each ripple spreads, an echo rare.
In belief, we find our strength anew,
Transforming shadows into light that's true.

The whispers of faith, soft and clear,
Invite us forward, dispelling fear.
As ripples widen, hearts will connect,
Building bridges in mutual respect.

Through storms and trials, we will stand,
With unified hearts, hand in hand.
For every ripple harbors a tale,
Of hope and belief in skies that prevail.

So let us cast our dreams like stones,
Creating ripples, breaking worn bones.
In this tapestry of life we weave,
Together in faith, we shall achieve.

Flowing Bonds

In gentle streams we find our way,
A light that guides through night and day.
With laughter shared and whispers sweet,
Our hearts entwined, a bond complete.

Through every storm that comes our way,
Together strong, we choose to stay.
Like rivers merging, flowing free,
Your soul is home, you're part of me.

With every tide, we rise and fall,
In moments small, we share it all.
From quiet times to loud delight,
Our flowing bonds, a beautiful sight.

As seasons change and years unfold,
Our story weaves, a thread of gold.
Through joys and trials, we've grown wise,
In each embrace, love never dies.

So let us stroll through time and space,
Hand in hand, we'll find our place.
In flows of life, we shall believe,
Together strong, we will achieve.

The Rhythm of Reliability

In every heartbeat, trust is found,
A steady pulse, a loving sound.
When shadows fall and doubts arise,
Your constancy, my peaceful skies.

Through every storm that shakes the night,
Your presence brings a calming light.
In whispered words or silent glance,
Reliability, our dance.

With every promise, firm and true,
A melody of me and you.
In laughter shared and burdens borne,
The rhythm thrives, forever sworn.

In times of doubt, when paths are rough,
Your arms, a haven, warm and tough.
With every challenge, we will stand,
Together strong, hand in hand.

So let us walk, side by side,
In harmony, our hearts will guide.
With every step, our love will shine,
The rhythm of a bond divine.

Depths of Devotion

In oceans wide, your love runs deep,
A treasure found, a promise keep.
Through waves that crash and tides that turn,
In depths of devotion, my heart will yearn.

With each sweet glance, our souls ignite,
A fire that burns through darkest night.
In quiet moments, our hearts align,
In this sacred space, your hand in mine.

Through every trial, together we stand,
With courage fierce, we face the land.
In storms that threaten, we shall prevail,
In depths of devotion, we won't fail.

Your laughter dances on the breeze,
A balm that flows through life's unease.
In whispered vows, our dreams take flight,
Together soaring, hearts alight.

So here we are, forever bound,
In every heartbeat, love profound.
In depths of devotion, we find our way,
Together always, come what may.

Surfing Serenity

On waves that crest, we ride with glee,
A dance of freedom, wild and free.
With salty air and sunlit skies,
In surfing serenity, the spirit flies.

The ocean calls, a soothing song,
In every swell, where we belong.
With laughter ringing, hearts in sync,
In every moment, we pause and think.

As tides will change, and winds will blow,
Together strong, we learn and grow.
In quiet coves or vibrant shores,
Surfing serenity, our souls explore.

Through sunlit days and starry nights,
In every wave, life feels just right.
With open hearts and minds unbound,
In surfing serenity, joy is found.

So let us ride where waters flow,
With passion bright, we'll take it slow.
In every wave and every spree,
Together we'll find our harmony.

The Quiet Song of Loyalty

In shadows deep, we pledge our hearts,
A bond unbroken, never parts.
Through storm and calm, we stand as one,
A silent song, when day is done.

With whispered vows upon the breeze,
No need for words, our spirits ease.
In every glance, a timeless trust,
In loyalty, we find our rust.

Through trials faced, we stand our ground,
In each small triumph, love is found.
A sturdy oak, in roots we tie,
Together strong, we reach the sky.

When shadows loom, we light the way,
In every night, we find the day.
A quiet strength forever binds,
In loyalty, our heart unwinds.

So here we sing, in harmony,
Of bonds that last, eternally.
Where loyalty flows, like rivers wide,
In every heart, love shall abide.

The Light Beyond the Dunes

Golden sands stretch far and wide,
Where shadows dance and dreams abide.
A whispered breeze carries the sound,
Of secrets kept beneath the ground.

O'er rolling dunes, the sun will rise,
A painted sky, in softest sighs.
With every step, a tale unfolds,
Of quiet strength and glimmers bold.

The ocean calls, its waves align,
With every crest, a spark divine.
Between the sands, hope finds a way,
To chase the dark and greet the day.

A lighthouse stands, guiding the lost,
Reminding us of dreams embossed.
In each soft grain, the past resides,
The light beyond where peace abides.

So let the dawn paint all the skies,
As in this journey, love complies.
With every step, embrace the view,
The light beyond, forever true.

Sailing on Serene Seas

The ocean's breath whispers of ease,
As we embark on tranquil seas.
With sails unfurled, we chase the sun,
In harmony, our hearts are one.

The waters gleam, a sapphire hue,
Beneath the sky of endless blue.
Each wave a song, a gentle tune,
We sail together, hearts immune.

With every gust, our spirits rise,
In every cloud, potential lies.
The horizon calls, it beckons us,
In this vast realm, we place our trust.

When storms may brew, we stand our ground,
With courage strong, our strength is found.
In every challenge, we find our grace,
Together, navigating space.

So raise the sails, let dreams take flight,
In moonlit paths, we'll find the light.
With hearts united, we roam the seas,
Sailing on, with utmost ease.

Threads of Interconnectedness

In every heart, a thread is spun,
A tapestry where lives are one.
Weaving stories, hand in hand,
Together strong, we make our stand.

The ties that bind are silent songs,
In love and laughter, where we belong.
From different paths, we find our way,
In every moment, come what may.

Through joys and sorrows, lace entwined,
In every soul, connection's kind.
With every echo, every cheer,
We find the strength to conquer fear.

With open hearts, we share the space,
In unity, we find our grace.
The threads of life, a vibrant hue,
In every bond, a vision true.

So let us dance in circles wide,
Embracing change, with arms open wide.
Together flowing, like rivers blend,
In threads of love, our lives transcend.

The Gathering Storm of Belief

Whispers rise in the shadowed night,
Hearts quicken with an unseen fright.
Shadows dance across the moor,
A restless tide begins to roar.

Sparks of hope ignite within,
Strength emerges, the will to begin.
In the chaos, clarity seeks,
A chorus loud, the spirit speaks.

Clouds collide in tempest's wake,
Each heartbeat, a promise we make.
Desire fuels the fire's gleam,
Together we forge a brighter dream.

Yet in the thunder, doubt may dwell,
But rise we must, to break the spell.
The storm may rage, but we will stand,
United souls, a steadfast band.

Through the tempest, belief will steer,
A beacon bright, it draws us near.
With courage, we will weather the night,
In the storm's embrace, we find our light.

Emulating the Ocean's Embrace

Waves caress the sunlit shore,
Endless love, forevermore.
Tides that pull with gentle grace,
Nature's arms, a warm embrace.

Salted air fills every breath,
Whispers soft as life and death.
Each wave a song, a soothing balm,
In its rhythm, we find calm.

Seagulls dance upon the breeze,
Nature's call in swaying trees.
Harmony in every crest,
The ocean's heart, our sacred quest.

As waters blend in twilight's glow,
Moonlit paths where dreams may flow.
Emulating love's sweet sound,
In the depths, our souls are found.

The ocean's pulse, a distant beat,
Calls us home with its retreat.
Boundless love that never wanes,
In its arms, we break our chains.

Sanctuaries of Safety

Within the heart, a secret place,
Where peace resides, wrapped in grace.
Sheltered dreams, where fears subside,
In this haven, we confide.

Whispers echo in gentle light,
Comfort found in the soft twilight.
Embrace of trust, a binding thread,
A sanctuary where hope is fed.

Hands clasped tight, we stand as one,
Facing storms until they're done.
Through struggles and trials, side by side,
In this refuge, love won't hide.

Together we weave a tapestry strong,
Where souls can rest, where we belong.
Each heartbeat nourished, each laugh shared,
In this sanctuary, we are cared.

From chaos, a new dawn shall rise,
With brighter days and open skies.
Sanctuaries of safety in our hearts,
Where every journey ever starts.

The Sound of Soft Waves

Listen close to the ocean's sigh,
As whispers weave beneath the sky.
Soft waves lap at the golden sand,
Caressing dreams with a gentle hand.

In the hush, there's a lullaby,
A serenade as time drifts by.
Each ripple carries a tale untold,
Of love and loss, both brave and bold.

Moonlit nights and starlit skies,
Reflections dance where silence lies.
In every crest, there's a mystery,
The ocean's heart beats endlessly.

Shores that shift with soft embrace,
Nature's art in timeless grace.
Listen close as the world unwinds,
In the sound, our solace finds.

So let the waves wash worries away,
In their rhythm, we'll choose to stay.
For in this calm, we come alive,
With every wave, our spirits thrive.

The Weaving of Reliability

In the loom of time, threads entwine,
Interwoven stories, a fabric fine.
Trust is the needle, precise and true,
Binding our hearts, me to you.

Every promise a stitch, every word a weave,
Crafting a tapestry we believe.
Under the surface, patterns unfold,
In the warmth of the trust that we hold.

When shadows whisper doubt and fear,
The strength of our bond will draw us near.
With every challenge, we grow anew,
Each strand a reminder of what we do.

We stand together, a fortress strong,
In the gentle rhythm of a shared song.
Reliability, a gift we embrace,
In the weaving of life, we find our place.

Through tempest and calm, the threads remain,
A tapestry bright, through joy and pain.
In this sacred fabric, we find our might,
The weaving of reliability, our guiding light.

Infinite Horizons of Hope

Beyond the mountains, where dreams collide,
Infinite horizons stretch far and wide.
Hope paints the sky with colors bright,
In the dawn of each new light.

Through valleys deep and rivers wide,
Hope is the current, the timeless guide.
With every step, we chase the dawn,
Infinite horizons draw us on.

In the quiet whispers of the breeze,
Hope lingers softly, putting hearts at ease.
It lifts our spirits, makes our spirits soar,
A beacon of promise, we can't ignore.

Together we wander, hand in hand,
On this journey, we take a stand.
With open hearts, our dreams unfold,
Infinite horizons, a story told.

Every sunset brings a hopeful new start,
In the tapestry of life, woven from the heart.
With every tomorrow, our spirits cope,
In the infinite horizons of hope.

Unseen Roots of Trust

Deep beneath the surface, roots intertwine,
Unseen connections, silently align.
Trust grows quietly, like a hidden tree,
In the fertile ground where we chose to be.

Through storms endured and seasons passed,
The strength of our bond, forever will last.
In shadows and light, our roots dig deep,
Nurturing promises, forever we keep.

Though winds may change and times may shift,
Our trust remains, an eternal gift.
In the heart of the forest, we find our way,
Unseen roots guide us, come what may.

As branches stretch out, reaching for skies,
The unseen roots hold where our spirit lies.
With every heartbeat, we stand side by side,
In the unseen roots of trust, we abide.

Together we flourish, through seasons we grow,
Fostering faith in the love we show.
In each other's arms, our spirits adjust,
Bound by the unseen roots of trust.

Currents of Companionship

In the river of life, we float as two,
Currents of companionship guiding us through.
Side by side, we navigate the bends,
With laughter and love, each moment transcends.

The waters may churn, and storms may arise,
Yet in each other, we find our skies.
Through ripples and waves, our bond remains strong,
In the currents of companionship, we belong.

With every challenge, we rise and we fall,
Together we weather, together we call.
The journey is richer when shared with a friend,
Currents of companionship that never end.

In the calm and the chaos, we find our way,
The laughter, the tears blend together each day.
In this flowing dance, our spirits ignite,
Currents of companionship shining so bright.

As we drift through the seasons, forever entwined,
In the tapestry of friendship, our hearts aligned.
Through all of life's waters, we endlessly roam,
In the currents of companionship, we've found our home.

A Symphony of Shared Secrets

In whispers soft beneath the stars,
Two hearts entwined, no fears, no bars.
Each secret shared, a quiet song,
In harmony, where we belong.

Through night's embrace, our dreams take flight,
In shadows dark, we find our light.
With every note, our souls unite,
Creating magic, pure and bright.

The universe spins, a tapestry,
Woven with threads of you and me.
A symphony of laughs and tears,
Echoing through the passing years.

In silent moments, truths unfold,
Stories told in gestures bold.
With every glance, a tale is spun,
In the symphony, we are one.

As dawn approaches, secrets stay,
In memory's realm, they gently sway.
Two hearts forever, a sacred pact,
A symphony, in love intact.

Twilight's Gentle Reassurance

Beneath the veil of softening light,
A tranquil world, day fades to night.
In twilight's arms, I find my peace,
A gentle calm, my worries cease.

Stars start to twinkle, one by one,
Whispering dreams, the day is done.
The moon ascends, a comforting glow,
Guiding my heart, where I must go.

The rustle of leaves in the evening breeze,
Carries my thoughts with perfect ease.
Each twilight moment, a fleeting sigh,
Wrapped in hope, as shadows fly.

The night unfolds with stories vast,
Echoes of whispers from the past.
In twilight's grace, I feel secure,
For in this stillness, I endure.

As darkness deepens, I close my eyes,
Embraced by night, where comfort lies.
Twilight, my keeper, I trust you so,
In your warm light, I choose to grow.

Gardens of Certainty

In gardens lush, where flowers bloom,
Each petal sings, dispelling gloom.
Roots intertwined, in earth they hold,
A tapestry of colors bold.

The sun on high, its warmth bestowed,
Nurturing life through paths we strode.
Each leaf whispers, secrets shared,
In every corner, love declared.

Seasons change, yet truth remains,
Through summer's heat and winter's rains.
In certainty, our hearts reside,
In each garden, hope won't hide.

Winding paths through foliage deep,
Where promises made, we safely keep.
In this haven, we find our way,
Together stronger, come what may.

Gardens of love, forever thrive,
In their embrace, we feel alive.
Through every storm, they stand so proud,
In certainty, our souls are crowd.

Flowing with Grace

Rivers dance in silver streams,
Flowing softly through our dreams.
A gentle current, a soothing pace,
Life abundant, flowing with grace.

The trees lean down to share a word,
In whispers sweet, their voices heard.
With every branch, we learn to trace,
A journey bold, flowing with grace.

Clouds drift by with tales untold,
Their shadows cast on meadows gold.
In nature's arms, we find our place,
Embraced by love, flowing with grace.

Mountains high and valleys wide,
In their presence, we can abide.
Through every trial, each fear we face,
We rise above, flowing with grace.

So let us dance like leaves in air,
Embrace the wind, without a care.
In every moment, find the space,
To simply be, flowing with grace.

Cascading Convictions

Rushing waters roar and dive,
In the depths, our truths contrive.
Each wave a thought that breaks away,
Shaping shores where dreams may stay.

Strong and clear, the current flows,
Through thick and thin, our spirit grows.
Cascades whisper secrets bold,
In every splash, a story told.

Roots of hope in rocky beds,
Where fear once ruled, now courage spreads.
Beliefs that buoy through stormy skies,
In flowing faith, our future lies.

With every drop, we feel the sway,
Lessons learned in a grand ballet.
Convictions strong, like ancient stone,
Guide us home, never alone.

The Horizon of Honor

Beneath the skies where dreams ignite,
A beacon shines, a steadfast light.
Guiding hearts through shadows cast,
To the horizon, loyalty vast.

In whispered winds, our values stand,
Together forged, hand in hand.
Each sunrise bold, each sunset clear,
Echoes of honor draw us near.

Mountains rise, but we are strong,
In unity, we all belong.
Though distant lands may call our name,
In the heart, we keep the flame.

Chasing visions, we won't relent,
In every trial, our will is spent.
For on this path of growth and pride,
The horizon shines, our guide, our tide.

Driftwood of Dependability

Washed ashore from distant seas,
Driftwood graces with its ease.
Nature's art in weathered form,
A silent vow, a shelter warm.

Among the tides, it stands secure,
In shifting sands, steadfast and pure.
With every storm that tries to break,
It bends but never does forsake.

Lessons carved by time's embrace,
Each ring a tale, a trace of grace.
In its strength, we find our ground,
A bond of trust that knows no bound.

Through sunlit days and moonlit nights,
It holds the stories of life's flights.
A guide that we can lean upon,
In driftwood's heart, the light lives on.

Soothing Swells

Gentle waves that kiss the shore,
Whispers soft, a tranquil lore.
In every swell, a lullaby,
Embracing all who drift nearby.

Moonlit dances on the crest,
A soothing balm, our souls at rest.
Rippling dreams in liquid hue,
Every tide a promise new.

The ocean's breath, a calming sigh,
An endless serenade, oh my!
In ebb and flow, we find our peace,
Where worries fade, and fears release.

Each sunset paints a canvas bright,
A symphony of day and night.
In soothing swells, we are renewed,
By nature's grace, our spirits queued.

Tides of Belief

Waves crash upon the shore,
Whispers of what lies in store.
Each crest a thought to embrace,
Each trough a silent space.

In the depths, hopes reside,
Flowing strong, like ocean tide.
Trust that ebbs and flows anew,
A journey shared by me and you.

Stars above, guiding light,
In the dark, they shine so bright.
With every shift, dreams can soar,
A promise of so much more.

In the tides, we find our way,
Through murky waters, come what may.
With courage, we'll set our sail,
A heart's resolve will never fail.

Along the shore, we leave our trace,
Imprints of our hopeful grace.
Tides of belief, they pull and weave,
In the embrace of all we believe.

Currents of Faith

In the stream of morning light,
We find our course, our inner sight.
Currents strong, but we are brave,
Riding waves, learning to save.

Through the rapids, doubts will flow,
Yet like rivers, we learn to grow.
With every bend, trust takes the lead,
In our hearts, we plant the seed.

Mountains high, valleys deep,
In this journey, we must leap.
Faith's embrace, a steady hand,
Guiding us to a promised land.

In stillness, we hear the call,
Echoes of strength that never fall.
Currents of faith, a steadfast friend,
On this path that has no end.

As branches sway and waters part,
We find solace, we speak heart.
With the current, spirits fly,
In faith's embrace, we touch the sky.

Undercurrents of Assurance

Beneath the waves, a force unseen,
Gently guiding, calm and keen.
In the depths, certainty thrives,
Undercurrents, where hope arrives.

With every ripple, whispers swirl,
In the ocean's depths, thoughts unfurl.
Through shifting sands, we must be wise,
Realizing strength never lies.

Tides may change, but trust remains,
In the heart, comfort sustains.
With every wave, we draw near,
In assurance, we have no fear.

Guided by compassion's grace,
We embrace our rightful place.
Undercurrents hold us tight,
In their warmth, there's endless light.

Through storms that rage and winds that shriek,
Our spirits shine, we will not break.
For even in the darkest night,
Undercurrents lead to light.

The Sea of Confidence

Together we sail on a vast sea,
Where confidence blooms, wild and free.
Each wave a push, a vibrant call,
To rise above and never fall.

With sails outstretched, we chase the sun,
In this dance, we are all one.
The horizon beckons, bright and clear,
In the sea of confidence, we steer.

Gentle tides cradle our dreams,
In the quiet, our spirit beams.
Boundless blue, a canvas wide,
In this journey, we take pride.

Through stormy skies and tranquil days,
We navigate in myriad ways.
With a compass forged in belief,
Confidence grants us sweet relief.

As stars align and guide our fate,
We recognize it's never too late.
The sea of confidence sings our song,
In its arms, we forever belong.

The Hidden Depths of Faith

In shadows deep where silence reigns,
A whisper calls through all the pains.
Roots embedded, unseen they grow,
Faith's gentle light begins to glow.

Through trials fierce, the heart will find,
Strength woven in the ties that bind.
With every tear, a promise waits,
Hope unfolds and never hesitates.

When storms arise and doubts collide,
A quiet trust will be our guide.
In unseen realms, the spirit soars,
A spirit free, it knows no doors.

With courage drawn from deep within,
Each step we take, a chance to begin.
For hidden jewels in faith's embrace,
Reveal the beauty of divine grace.

Patterns in the Sand

Footprints dance on shores so wide,
Each a story, where hearts abide.
Waves will wash some memories clear,
While others linger, ever near.

In twilight hues, the patterns fade,
Yet in our hearts, the echoes stayed.
A fleeting glance, a whispered name,
The grains of time, they know no shame.

Through shifting tides, we leave our mark,
In fleeting moments caught in spark.
As sunlit dreams weave through the night,
We trace our hopes in soft daylight.

Though sand may shift, our bonds remain,
In every loss, there is a gain.
The patterns drawn in love's embrace,
Will always find our destined place.

Currents Beneath a Moonlit Sky

The river flows, a silver thread,
Beneath the stars where dreams are fed.
Whispers float on gentle waves,
As moonlight dances, darkness braves.

In quiet depths, the secrets lie,
Hidden truths that never die.
With every ripple, stories wake,
The heartbeats echo, choices make.

Through midnight hours, we seek and search,
For guiding lights in nature's church.
The currents strong, yet calm and wise,
Lead us gently to the skies.

Reflections cast in shimmering light,
Remind us of our inner fight.
For every shadow, there's a spark
To light our way through the dark.

Sails Filled with Assurance

The winds arise, a call so bold,
Sails unfurl, the stories told.
With steady hands, we grip the line,
Trust the journey, all will align.

Through tempest skies, we face the gales,
Eyes on horizons where hope prevails.
Each wave a challenge, strong and fierce,
Yet in our hearts, the fear we pierce.

With every gust, our spirits soar,
Navigating to distant shores.
With courage deep, our hearts set free,
The ocean's vast, our destiny.

As stars will guide through darkest nights,
The sails will catch what trust ignites.
Hand in hand, through windswept dreams,
Together, we'll chase the sun's bright beams.

The Whisper of Promises

In shadows soft, they gently float,
A quiet vow, a tender note.
The moonlit path, where dreams align,
In whispered tones, your hand in mine.

Through valleys low, and mountains high,
We chase the stars, we touch the sky.
Each promise held, like fog on glass,
In every moment, we shall pass.

The pulse of time, a gentle rhyme,
In silence shared, we dance with prime.
An echo formed from hearts that yearn,
A flame of hope, in trust we burn.

Beneath the weight of evening's shroud,
We find our strength; we say it loud.
For every promise, long or brief,
Brings peace to hearts, and sweet relief.

With every breath, we weave our tale,
In breezes soft, we will not fail.
The whispers dance, a perfect art,
Bound by the love within our heart.

Currents of Connection

In tides that rise, we find our way,
A bond unseen, yet bright as day.
Through every wave, we turn and sway,
In currents deep, we long to stay.

Each gentle pull, a silent call,
A dance of souls, we rise, we fall.
In currents strong, we lose the fight,
Yet find our peace in the fading light.

The bridges built from dreams we share,
In every glance, a spark of care.
The ties of trust, they bind us deep,
In whispers low, our promises keep.

As rivers flow, we journey forth,
Discovering new, and valuing worth.
The currents shift, yet still we blend,
In this vast sea, our hearts transcend.

Together we sail, 'neath skies so wide,
In the heart's boat, we choose to ride.
Through storms and calm, our spirits soar,
In currents of love, forevermore.

The Lighthouse of Faithfulness

In storms that rage, a beacon stands,
Its guiding light, through shifting sands.
With every wave that crashes down,
It whispers hope, dispels the frown.

The steadfast glow, through darkest night,
A promise kept, to guide our sight.
Though tempests roar, and shadows creep,
In faithfulness, our souls will leap.

The chirping birds at break of dawn,
Will sing a tune, the night withdrawn.
Each flicker beams, a warmth we crave,
In faithful hearts, we find the brave.

Through rocky shores and whispered winds,
The flame of trust, it never thins.
Each lighthouse stands, a tale of grace,
In every heart, you'll find a place.

So let us sail, where waters gleam,
With faithfulness our constant theme.
The lighthouse guides, in joy or strife,
Forever bright, it shapes our life.

Ripples of Understanding

In quiet depths, the waters flow,
With gentle touch, we come to know.
Each ripple formed, a thought set free,
In calm embraces, you and me.

Through eyes that speak, we dare to see,
The world anew, in harmony.
Where hearts can share, their silent screams,
In ripples soft, we weave our dreams.

The currents shift, but still we stay,
Transcending time, in every way.
With empathy, our spirits blend,
In ripples deep, the hearts we mend.

We lift our souls, in truth we stand,
Creating peace, a healing hand.
In every smile, a bridge we build,
With ripples wide, our hearts are filled.

So side by side, we'll always flow,
In understandings that softly grow.
Through every moment, hand in hand,
We'll dance in ripples across the land.

Streams of Unwavering Support

In times of need, we stand so near,
A whispering strength that calms all fear.
Like rivers flowing, deep and wide,
Together we rise, side by side.

Through storms that rage, through skies so gray,
We find the light, we find our way.
With every challenge, we hold tight,
Together we shine, a guiding light.

In laughter shared, in silent cries,
We weave our bonds, where trust still lies.
In every moment, a truth so pure,
In hearts aligned, we find the cure.

From tides of doubt, we break away,
With hands held high, we greet the day.
Through trials faced, our spirits soar,
In streams of love, we find the shore.

Forever forward, we'll chart the course,
In every trial, we uncover force.
With every heartbeat, we reassure,
Our streams of support forever endure.

The Longitude of Loyalty

In every moment, we stand aligned,
A measure of trust, so well-defined.
Through every trial, through joy and strife,
Loyalty weaves the fabric of life.

With every whisper, a promise made,
In shadows cast, our fears will fade.
Together strong through night and day,
In loyalty's heart, we find our way.

As stars adorn the velvet skies,
Our bond unbroken, as time flies.
From shores of silence, to oceans wide,
In every pulse, our truths abide.

Through shifting paths and winding roads,
Our loyalty strong, is love's true abode.
In every heartbeat, through every tear,
A longitude measured, forever near.

So let the world around us change,
Our faithful hearts will still remain.
In every challenge, in all we trust,
With loyalty's lens, we rise and adjust.

Murmurs in the Wind

The gentle breeze carries sweet refrain,
Soft whispers echo, like falling rain.
In twilight's glow, secrets align,
Murmurs in the wind, a sacred sign.

With every rustle, a tale unfolds,
Of dreams untold and hearts so bold.
In every sigh, the earth reveals,
Murmurs in the wind, our fate it seals.

Through forests deep and seas that roar,
The winds of change open every door.
They guide us forth, through dusk and dawn,
Revealing paths that stretch beyond.

In quiet valleys, on mountain high,
Murmurs in the wind, a lullaby.
They carry wishes, hopes, and fears,
In their soft cadence, life appears.

So listen closely, with open hearts,
To nature's choir, where magic starts.
In every gust, let your spirit tend,
To the soft whispers, the wind's sweet blend.

Sailing Through Shadows

In silent waters, the shadows play,
We sail the seas at the close of day.
With courage steady, the sail unfurled,
We navigate an uncertain world.

Each gust of wind tells tales of old,
Of dreams adrift and hearts so bold.
Through storms that rise, through skies so dim,
We chart our course, on hope we swim.

The stars above light our long way home,
In darkest hours, we still will roam.
With every wave, we learn to trust,
Sailing through shadows, as we must.

In quiet moments, we find our grace,
With every heartbeat, we embrace.
Though shadows linger, we will not wane,
Through trials faced, we've much to gain.

So let the wind carry us afar,
Our journey guided by each bright star.
For sailing through shadows, the brave will see,
That light will follow where hearts are free.

Shifting Sands of Assurance

In the desert's embrace, we find our way,
With whispers of hope guiding each day.
Footprints in the sand, a reminder so clear,
Trust in the journey, for solace is near.

Winds may erode what we thought was secure,
Yet in every storm, our hearts remain pure.
Like grains that shift, we adapt and reshape,
Finding our strength in the vast, open space.

Each moment a lesson, the past slips away,
Through trials and triumphs, we learn to stay.
Embracing the change, we rise and we fall,
In the shifting sands, we discover it all.

Beneath the stars, we gather our dreams,
In nights full of wonder, nothing's as it seems.
With courage, we stand on the edge of the night,
Knowing with assurance, we'll step into light.

So hold fast your faith in this uncertain land,
For together we walk, hand in hand.
Amidst the changing tides, let love be our guide,
In the shifting sands, let hope abide.

Beyond the Horizon of Faith

As dawn breaks the horizon, dreams take their flight,
With colors of promise igniting the night.
We reach for tomorrow, where shadows recede,
With faith as our compass, we plant every seed.

In valleys of doubt, where silence can scream,
We navigate storms, fueled by a dream.
Horizons may beckon, but we bravely stand,
With courage ignited, united we land.

Though clouds may gather, and fears may enthrall,
A beacon of hope will guide through it all.
We rise with each sunrise, casting aside,
The whispers of doubt in the heart's deep inside.

For every step forward, a moment of grace,
We challenge the shadows, we run life's embrace.
Beyond every struggle, the light will gleam bright,
With faith in tomorrow, we'll soar into light.

So trust in the journey, believe in the way,
Embrace all the wonders that come with each day.
Beyond the horizon, together we chase,
The beauty of faith, a boundless space.

Serene Waters of Commitment

In the stillness of dusk, reflections abound,
Serene waters whisper, a soft, calming sound.
Promises echo on the surface so clear,
In the depths of our hearts, commitment draws near.

Ripples may form but will soon fade away,
As love's gentle currents, together we sway.
With steadfast devotion, we build and we grow,
In the tranquil embrace, our true feelings show.

Each glance, a reminder of vows that we've made,
Through seasons of change, in sun or in shade.
In the harmony found, we dance to our song,
With passion and purpose, where we both belong.

As stars paint the night, our hearts intertwine,
In the serene waters, your soul flows with mine.
Together we navigate the tides of this life,
United in love, as husband and wife.

So let us hold tightly to what we have sworn,
In the calm of our bond, our spirits reborn.
For in these serene waters, we find our way,
With commitment as deep as the dawn of the day.

Currents of Connection

Across the vast ocean, our souls intertwine,
In the currents of connection, our hearts align.
With every small gesture, a bridge we create,
Uniting our spirits, as we resonate.

Like rivers that flow, we wander and glide,
In the depths of our laughter, we let joy reside.
Each ripple a moment, each wave a new chance,
To cherish the magic found in this dance.

Through storms that may come, hand in hand we stand,
Facing the tide with a love that's so grand.
With courage we navigate the ebbs and the flows,
In the currents of life, our connection still grows.

The whispers of friendship, the warmth of a smile,
In the currents we travel, let's stay for a while.
For every heartbeat shared, a bond is renewed,
In the depths of connection, our love is imbued.

So let's sail together through calm and through storm,
For in each other's arms, we find our true form.
In life's flowing river, through laughter and tears,
In the currents of connection, we'll conquer our fears.

The Confluence of Trust

In the quiet of the night,
Whispers weave with the stars,
Hearts align in gentle light,
Faith blooms, erasing scars.

Hands that guide through the storm,
Anchors in turbulent seas,
Together, we will transform,
As trust's warm embrace frees.

Paths interlaced as we stride,
Each step nurtures the bond,
In the dance where souls collide,
We're a melody, beyond.

To build a fortress of grace,
With pillars strong as time,
Even shadows find their place,
In this symphony, we climb.

Through the valleys, we will soar,
Guided by the light we share,
In unity, we restore,
The power of trust laid bare.

Whispered Promises

Beneath the moon's soft glow,
Vows hang like morning dew,
In the silence, love will flow,
Whispers shared between us two.

Every secret softly held,
In the twilight's tender grace,
In this bond, we are compelled,
To find joy in every place.

Promises tied with a thread,
Worn like jewels in our hearts,
In each word, a dream is bred,
A canvas where love imparts.

When the storms begin to rise,
And the shadows stretch and sway,
Trusting in our silent ties,
We'll find hope to light the way.

No distance can break our song,
Through the trials, we will stand,
In this promise, we belong,
Together, hand in hand.

Rhythms of Support

In the chorus of our plight,
Harmony in hearts we find,
With each note, we share our fight,
Resonating, intertwined.

Gentle hands, a steady beat,
Lifting dreams when spirits fall,
In the dance, we won't retreat,
Together, we will stand tall.

When the world feels out of tune,
And shadows begin to play,
We'll compose beneath the moon,
A rhythm guiding the way.

Echoes of our laughter rise,
In the winds of hope and cheer,
Strength and love become our prize,
In each moment, we draw near.

So let the music unfold,
As we write our life's refrain,
With every story ever told,
Support is our lasting gain.

Beneath the Surface of Doubt

In the depths where shadows creep,
Thoughts swirl like a restless tide,
In silence, secrets often seep,
Yet truth is where hope will bide.

Brave the currents, face the fears,
In the chaos, clarity grows,
As we gather up our tears,
Courage blooms, and wisdom flows.

Beneath the weight of heavy hearts,
Resilience gently unfurls,
Through the struggle, beauty starts,
Lighting paths across our worlds.

In the stillness, doubts may speak,
Yet within them lies the spark,
For the journey, strong and meek,
Can illuminate the dark.

So let us dive beyond the veil,
Seek the treasures hidden deep,
Together, we will not derail,
In this bond, our spirits leap.

The Quiet Power of Unison

In whispers soft, the hearts align,
A silent bond, a path divine.
Together strong, we forge our way,
In quiet power, we choose to stay.

With every step, in harmony,
We lift our spirits, wild and free.
In unison, our voices blend,
A tapestry of love we send.

Through trials faced, we stand as one,
In darkest nights, we find the sun.
The quiet strength that we possess,
In unity, we find our best.

Each heartbeat echoes, firm and true,
In gentle grace, we carry through.
The world may roar, but we remain,
Bound by the peace that breaks the chain.

Together forged, our souls ignite,
In whispered dreams, we find our light.
The quiet power of unison,
Together, we have just begun.

Timeless Tides of Friendship

Friendship flows like ocean's tide,
In every wave, love does reside.
Through storms and calm, we rise and fall,
A timeless bond, we share it all.

In laughter's echo, we find our joy,
An unbroken trust no storm can destroy.
With open hearts, we face the day,
Through every challenge, come what may.

Seasons change, yet we remain,
In sunlit skies or soothing rain.
The tides may churn, but we hold fast,
A friendship built to truly last.

With every sunrise, new dreams to chase,
In timeless tides, we find our place.
Together navigating life's expanse,
In every moment, we take a chance.

A treasure found in each shared glance,
In every heartbeat, a sacred dance.
Timeless tides, we'll ride till end,
For life's rich journey, we are friends.

Horizons Painted with Trust

Upon the canvas, colors gleam,
Horizons bright, a shared dream.
With every stroke, our hopes arise,
In trust we find a sweet surprise.

Together stepping into the light,
Guided by faith, futures bright.
Each moment cherished, we create,
A masterpiece that won't abate.

In skies of gold and shades of blue,
We paint a world that feels so true.
Through every trial, hand in hand,
In unity, we dream and stand.

With love as strong as mountains high,
We reach for stars in the endless sky.
Horizons stretch both wide and far,
In every heartbeat, you're my star.

Together we'll embrace the dawn,
In painted hues, our fears are gone.
Horizons vast, forever free,
In trust, we find our destiny.

Celestial Reflections

Beneath the moon's soft, silver glow,
The stars above begin to show.
Celestial whispers fill the night,
In reflections deep, we find our light.

The cosmos dances, a timeless view,
Galaxies twirl in shades of blue.
Each twinkling star, a dream entwined,
In silent echoes, our hearts aligned.

In every shadow, a story told,
Of love and hope, both brave and bold.
Celestial wonders guide our way,
In silent prayers, we find our sway.

With every heartbeat, rhythms blend,
In starry skies, our worries mend.
Reflections bright in a cosmic sea,
Together, we unfold our destiny.

As dawn approaches, the night must fade,
In love's embrace, our dreams are made.
Celestial reflections, pure and vast,
In every moment, our spirits cast.

www.ingramcontent.com/pod-product-compliance
Ingram Content Group UK Ltd.
Pitfield, Milton Keynes, MK11 3LW, UK
UKHW021643200125
4187UKWH00003B/258

9 781805 602859